THE CLOSING OF
The Rose

Carolyn Dunnett

THE CLOSING OF THE ROSE

Copyright © Carolyn Dunnett

The right of Carolyn Dunnett to be identified as the author of this work has been asserted by her in accordance with the Copyright, Designs and Patents Act 1988.

ISBN: 978-0-9562077-1-5

All rights reserved. No part of this publication may be reproduced or transmitted in any form or by any means, electronic or mechanical. Including photocopying, recording, or any information storage and retrieval system without permission in writing from the author.

British Library Cataloguing Data

A catalogue record of this book is available from The British Library

Published by Sealove Books
8 Southview Drive
Worthing BN11 5HU

Design and Typesetting by Verité CM Ltd

Printed in England

CONTENTS

Acknowledgements
1. THE CLOSING OF THE ROSE
2. WRITING
3. LAMPS
4. ENGLISH BREAKFAST TEA
5. ORIGINS
6. DURING A LULL
7. CONSEQUENCES
8. KITE SURFERS
9. BARN OWL
10. LEGACY
11. SECONDHAND BOOKSHOP
12. TWENTY-FIRST CENTURY EXODUS
13. THE SHELL TEMPLE, MARGATE
14. MILLENNIUM MUSINGS
15. ZILLERTALBAHN
16. A TURNER SPECTRUM
17. TOP POND, EXBURY GARDENS
18. THE ART OF MEDICINE – VIENNA 1796
19. MIAOW
20. SLIPPING AWAY
21. SONG OF LONGING
22. CAPTURED IN ST. IVES
23. DRINKS ANYONE?
24. THE LURE OF WATER
25. JEWISH MONUMENT (Vienna)
26. HYDE ESTATE (27th March)
27. APOLLO'S COLLAPSE
28. WHAT HAPPENED ON BOXING DAY

THE CLOSING OF THE ROSE

29. DREAMING
30. THE DIAMOND MUSEUM, BRUGES
31. THE BURNING EYE
32. SUMMER SNAPSHOT
33. "ALL THAT GLISTERS"
34. DOWN THE YARD
35. MARSH
36. THE FIRST CHRISTMAS
37. VICTIM
38. MEETING
39. ENDING
40. MIRACLE FLOWERS
41. PERUVIAN SCISSOR DANCE
42. DETECTIVE WORK
43. SEASCAPE
44. CAPILLA REAL
45. MAKE-UP GIRL
46. THE BEGINNINGS OF AN ADDICTION
47. REBIRTH
48. A MINUTE MYSTERY
49. ARIES, the Ram
50. TAURUS – the bull
51. GEMINI – the twins
52. CANCER – the crab
53. LEO – the lion
54. VIRGO – the virgin
55. LIBRA – the scales
56. SCORPIO – the scorpion
57. SAGITTARIUS – the archer
58. CAPRICORN – the goat
59. AQUARIUS – the water carrier
60. PISCES – the fish

THE CLOSING OF THE ROSE

61. PORTRAIT OF EDITH SITWELL
62. NO ANSWER
63. LIGHTHOUSE KEEPER
64. ARCTIC EXPLORER
65. JUNKIE
66. AFTERMATH
67. ELEMENTAL PRAYER
68. LANGUOR
69. CALLING ARTHUR
70. AUERSPERG CONCERT
71. DAYBREAK
72. SEA-SENSE
73. WAIL
74. IMPRINT
75. BLUE HILLS REMEMBERED
76. IN THE TEAHOUSE
77. DENIAL
78. GRANDAD'S WORKSHOP
79. HASTINGS
80. ARTFUL DODGER
81. EVENING MIST, HEIAN
82. COMING OUT
83. GREAT GRANDMA, LOUISA
84. NARRATIVE
85. WILDE GENIUS
86. NUDE BATHING
87. THE BIRTH OF VENUS (Botticelli)
88. RECIDIVIST
89. STAR CREDENTIALS
90. PEOPLE

ACKNOWLEDGEMENTS

My thanks to Toni, for her words of wisdom;
and to all the Posters.

1. THE CLOSING OF THE ROSE

Before the leafing of the bud,
come, take my hand;
unfold our lives together,
give me the bright green of your dreams.

Before the falling dew-drop dries,
enrich my thoughts with your wisdom;
nurture the love growing within.

Before the hardening of the thorn,
soften your wrath if I have hurt you.
Prevent annoyance turning to disdain.

Before the closing of the rose,
enfold me now against your satin core.
Desist from yearning or regret.

Before the cutting of the stem,
know I love you
beyond the longest silence,
and truly, when you drop, I'm lost.

2. WRITING

Drowning in thoughts, I clutch at nouns,
bend words to my will,
describe hurtful events,
sift the past.
Sometimes ideas block,
egg-timer fashion,
only to surge
months later.
Anywhere peaceful is suitable
to play with words,
record a baby's smile,
give your personal view.
Historians record globally,
miss personal poignant moments.
Joining the clan
of people of imagination,
I am drawn to write,
as gravity compels the sea.

THE CLOSING OF THE ROSE

3. LAMPS

AT NIGHT
IT TAKES
BUT LITTLE LIGHT
TO MAKE THE OUTLOOK
VERY BRIGHT
BUT
IF
BY
ILL
LUCK
THE
BULB
SHOULD
BLOW
YOU
LOSE
THE
GLOW
THEN DARK IS RESTFUL TOO YOU KNOW

4. ENGLISH BREAKFAST TEA

At 4am
incongruous among driftwood,
rope and stone,
a Thermos rests abandoned
at the tide-line;
not smashed by vigorous waves
but gently settled
in its resting place.

The two
who pledge each other,
not in champagne
but English Breakfast tea,
share between them
hospital vigils, many broken nights,
the small corpse
of a dearly cherished son.

They've huddled here all night,
released; but neither sea nor stars
can answer their eternal questioning.

5. ORIGINS

Born of the earth,
they discern it tugging
to keep their skittish
limbs from wandering.

Born of the fire,
their motion is writhing
across earth's surface
consuming, destroying.

Born of the air,
they relish its whirling,
with fitful eddies
gusting and returning.

Born of the sea,
I can feel its longing
to draw Earth's children
to its siren singing.

6. DURING A LULL

Breathless calm soothes me
to a deckchair doze.
Seahorses hang in their element
below surface
while my alien skin crinkles,
rubs sore.
People prattle on.
They don't know I've left them,
gone to where foam breaks and water moans.
With echoing sounds I float back,
Oh ... so ... slowly...

7. CONSEQUENCES

Begin with gin,
carouse, arouse,
explore; adore
your find, then bind.

Omit the wit,
regress, depress,
observe raw nerve,
imply a lie,
annoy, destroy;
kowtow, not now!

Affair. Despair,
get tough, rebuff,
diverge; emerge
before the law.
Recall, appal,
report, retort,
adore no more.

Divorce perforce,
dispute the loot;
remorse? – of course.

8. KITE SURFERS

The roof could lose slates in this wind,
Droves of kite-surfers assemble,
hefting rigs from rusty vans,
curtained secrets safely hidden.
Assembling them seems to need
interpreting a 3D instructional diagram.

Staggering against resistant water
they thrust off, try to stand.
Sail angled, they pierce air
like express trains,
appearing on far horizons.
Shooting back as meteors they grind pebbles,
tumble into the foam.
Wetsuits give a second skin
never needed pre-natally.
Tasting salt with every breath
they briefly outfly birds
with acrobatic loops and whorls
describing a perfect O,
whose twin emerges from the lips of onlookers.

Safely ensconced behind the café window,
we exhilarate,
share their triumphs.

9. BARN OWL

Owl glides silent
on mothy wings,
claws extended
at quick rustlings.
Unsuspecting mouse or vole
is captured and taken
through the nest-hole.
The chicks gasp
and hiss for food.
The male struggles
to feed his brood,
but the year is good.
They will both survive.
It won't take one
to keep the other alive.

10. LEGACY

Of course it isn't right, you must agree.
She's left it to a cat's home, in her will.
The family think it's all a travesty,

though Henry, Edna's son is filled with glee.
He knew the very thought would make me ill.
Of course it isn't right. You must agree.

I never will forgive his perfidy
in causing me to down this bitter pill.
The family think it's all a travesty.

We've fallen out. No hope of harmony!
He's wanting me to share the lawyer's bill.
Of course it isn't right, you must agree.

It seems to me a sad epitome
of life today. He schemed it with such skill.
The family think it's all a travesty.

Her legacy was promised just to me
and now at last I'll be receiving nil.
Of course it isn't right. You must agree.
The family think it's all a travesty.

11. SECONDHAND BOOKSHOP

The smell entices me,
like Grandad's old cigar-box.
Books a century old
sit yellowing in piles.
Inside, you can only sidle
quiet, between the stacks,
like tiptoeing on blotting-paper.
No wall is visible,
only stairways to heaven
of dusty, musty volumes
waiting to be rescued.
For the owner, each is a snatched jewel
to be hoarded and restored.
Lose yourself for an hour's bliss.
No cares will intrude.
All bookworms welcome!

THE CLOSING OF THE ROSE

12. TWENTY-FIRST CENTURY EXODUS

The dolphins surge ahead. We follow on
to try to gain our safety in a place
away from war. But mostly hope has gone.
We've drifted several days and still we face
the hostile waves that try to sink the boat.
A subtle murmur surges to a prayer
for anything to help us stay afloat,
or for a crewman to produce a flare.
Then suddenly a ship steams into view.
We raise a feeble cheer and try to shout.
They spot us and the sturdy British crew
soon manage to dispel our sense of doubt,
as one by one we're briskly hauled aboard
to travel somewhere else they call abroad.

13. THE SHELL TEMPLE, MARGATE

The sum of all knowledge is here,
Sun, Moon and stars;
Mother, Father, God;
procreation, the passage of life;
union with the Deity.

By day through the open dome
Ra rides to his rightful place.
Is this my soul's pathway to the stars
like the pyramids, or Angkor Wat?

Round the Rotunda in ritual procession,
through the winding passage in darkness,
only the moon lights our path
to the sanctuary.

Marvelling at the designs there,
in the smoky light of the conch lamps,
I pour libations,
lie prostrate before the Oracle,
hoping for answers.

14. MILLENNIUM MUSINGS

Two thousand years ago today
in Bethlehem, the Christ-child lay.
The Magi saw the Messiah's birth
that brought Love's message here, on earth.

And after these two thousand years,
what sets his followers apart?
Those people claiming faith, or none,
who act on Love within their heart.

15. ZILLERTALBAHN

Snorting like an inexperienced baby dragon,
a small steam engine
puffs us up the Zillertal.
With a final despairing hiss
it grinds to a halt halfway.
Wooden seats get harder by the minute
as we sit and wait,
while local voices establish
it has run out of water.

Heroes of the hour,
local fire-brigade ride to the rescue
on red-caparisoned charger.
For, in an exception to fairy-tales,
the dragon is not to be slain
but aided to recovery.
Until, with thirst quenched,
it can fire and steam
with due aplomb.

Meanwhile, like a catwalk model
it is winked at from all sides
by dozens of cameras.

16. A TURNER SPECTRUM

The first time
they had dared him.
"Only a pile of boxes in the alleyway.
Set them alight
and you can join our gang."

        Flames – prancing
        writhing, twirling
        flamenco dancers
        coming to a crescendo.

Next, the straw-stack.
He stood with the crowd
feigning surprise
at the inferno.

        Sparks – golden rain;
        showers
        from Versailles' fountains.

The tyre depot
was a mistake.
Not much to see

    except

        Smoke; surging,
        smothering,
        shepherding people
        hastily before it.

THE CLOSING OF THE ROSE

The wrecked car was better.
Blistering paint,
cracking of glass and hot metal.

        Heat – stunning, suffocating.
        He became as an ice-cube, melting
        its identity in the water-jug.

Lastly, the school blaze.
It had them all.
Flames, Sparks, Smoke, Heat, POWER
He had unleashed his hounds
to devour the neighbourhood.
He stood, entranced
by his handiwork.

        Colours – orange, red, crimson, yellow,
        purple; a Turner canvas of a sky ablaze.
        But the two large blue spots
        appearing to revolve before his eyes;
        they were not in his grand design.

Nor was the small stretchered figure
carried to the ambulance.
His mother asked
"Where's Billy? He went back to school to find you."

17. TOP POND, EXBURY GARDENS

Serene arrows in dappled sunlight,
fish circle and plunge
through green and orange reflections
to the pond's depths.

I sit serene by its edge,
mind moving freely,
soaring, not dredging depths,
reflecting on the day's beauty.

18. THE ART OF MEDICINE – VIENNA 1796

They feel behind my ears and round my skull
to gauge what I am thinking, for I'm mute.
White-surpliced priests, whose church financed this Hall,
have changed to dark-robed doctors, with the might
of Faith behind them. They espouse the views
of one, Franz Joseph Gall, who keeps me here
and daily reads my cranium; lays hands
on bumps and hollows underneath my hair.

The village that I came from has a pond.
Nearby, there lived a boy who disappeared,
to re-emerge a few days later, drowned.
By some mischance, the common view was aired
that I had killed him. Hopeless, to protest
without the power of speech! I loved him, true,
but not the way they thought. I cannot trust
my silent eloquence to get me free.

Incarcerated, studied all the time!
They're sure I'm guilty; wish to read my thoughts,
their fingers on my brain to map my mind.
The fabled truths of which Franz Joseph prates
will branch into a science at my expense.
Phrenology he calls it and he claims
ability to read my skull. He schemes
a living death for me, until I'm bones.

19. MIAOW

     so   as
his   ears
 sharp   as claws
    relax
   oozing
 contentment
before the blaze
   roundly
  balletic on
sideboards and
tables shamelessly   W
wanton to tickling   O
 fingers he revs   A
  his jet engine I
   unceasing M

20. SLIPPING AWAY

Sand grates my heels.
I've moved
from the thin towel I lie on.
Sunlight presses my eyelids
as coins on dead eyes.
But I am very much alive,
ready to slip out of my skin.
Breezes carry me above the waves
to dance with the gulls
and fly to far horizons.
I see tropical islands, palm trees,
coconuts and treasure chest;
a man digging to release it
from its tomb.
Drifting on, I watch tall sailing ships
hastening like racing-camels in the desert.
Hunger draws me back to reality,
to the laden cool-bag
I was determined not to breach
before twelve noon.

21. SONG OF LONGING

I long to soar like a bird,
to fly from trouble.
I long for peace,
with argument dead.
I long for health,
for freedom from pain,
from troubling thoughts
inside my head.

22. CAPTURED IN ST. IVES

Your dwellings stack card-style upon the hill,
in twisting alleys rub shoulders
like friends upon a couch.
All is up or down,
hard for unpractised feet, grinding
past Boutique cottages.
Ivy and small pink flowers smile welcome
from every crevice.

Peep through the Epidaurus Bronze
to the sweep of the bay; or linger
on the Harbour Hotel terrace
admiring the view,
to drink and possibly tell
of the Lantern Ghost who stalks the town.
Black rocks hold buildings
away from the water,
everywhere full of colour – harbour sand,
bright surfboards, the sea,
art which fills the shops.

If you were born here, it would surely
hold you prisoner for ever.
As it is, a tentacle circles my wrist!

23. DRINKS ANYONE?

Our birthdays seem to chase from year to year
no matter that we find the time for fun.
They have no sooner passed than they are here,

a wonderful excuse for drinking beer
especially at the age of twenty-one.
Our birthdays seem to chase from year to year.

As time moves on, we won't be cavalier
but harvest precious hours in unison.
They have no sooner passed than they are here.

It seems that time can simply disappear
but we're determined it shall run and run
yet birthdays seem to chase from year to year.

Now we will raise an energetic cheer
and drink a toast to every single one.
They have no sooner passed than they are here.

He's been Sir Lancelot to my Guinevere,
joint celebrant, delightful one-to-one.
Our birthdays seem to chase from year to year.
They have no sooner passed than they are here.

24. THE LURE OF WATER

Waves, like stirred coffee
curl playfully round beach rock-pools,
depositing crabs, for explorers
carrying buckets and nets.

Wellingtons love puddles,
jump and splash
of their own accord,
taking small owners with them.

On ponds,
woolly pom-pom ducklings
scrabble furiously in their mother's wake,
while pondskaters glide
between frogspawn and lilies.

Rocking to the rhythm
of rowing-boats,
lakes echo with laughter
of summer delights.

25. JEWISH MONUMENT
(Vienna)

We confront closed doors
carved in stone.
But those others were immoveable too.

And books
back-to-front, upside down
like the lives together lost in smoke.

Like an orange, flambé
the world's exposed.
All it takes is one maniac with a match.

26. HYDE ESTATE
(27th March)

Here I can sing my soul's song
in greenery, bright daffodils.

27. APOLLO'S COLLAPSE

Writhing wind wraps corners of the building.
Rain drips, counting out the seconds.
Fierce, furious gusts
collect drips into puddles, ponds even.
Expected December weather,
but not confined on a roof.
The audience, blissfully unaware,
is focussed only on the motion
of the play.
Then come strange sighs,
creaks and groans
as of a lost soul.
A sudden shout of warning
and pieces of the balcony break
showering those below.
Crashes and screams follow,
temporary fog of dust dervishes,
prostrate people,
ambulances.
These ancient buildings,
ornate plasterwork and all
are preserved within an inch of their life,
anybody's life.

28. WHAT HAPPENED ON BOXING DAY

The tide was very low, receding fast,
when Chanui did his usual chore and ran
as fast as he could go to dig for bait.
He took his wooden pail on which he'd scratched
his name some years ago, once he knew how.
But, as he skipped his way towards the tide,
he noticed something he'd not seen before,
some fish, like sprinters gasping on the sand.
Then, as he paused to catch his breath, he saw
a heave of water higher than their house.
It rushed at him and knocked him off his feet.
He fought for breath and thought that he would drown
but clawed his way up to the salty air.

No time for anyone to get away
before the great tsunami hit the shore.
The trees inland were pulled up from their roots
as easily as hairs plucked from the chin.
And when the tide had come and gone again
the fishing-village boats and houses lay
like Chanui's toys upended on the floor,
though smashed to pieces by a giant boot.
No streets were visible and what remained
were shattered heaps of debris, filled with spears.

THE CLOSING OF THE ROSE

The lone man who surveyed the wreckage there
was Chanui's father, who had searched all day
to find his son, and slumped exhausted now.
His hands were raw from handling wet wood
and other debris he had tugged aside,
his throat as sore from shouting Chanui's name
as if he'd swallowed mouthfuls of the sand.
The neighbours had all fled to higher ground
and he began to fear his strength had gone.

His heart was filled with anger for he knew
that what gave him his livelihood had robbed
him of his son.
He felt as though his heart would never mend.
Before the darkness came, he made his way
to find clean water that was fit to drink.
He thought it would sustain him for next day.
He struggled, stumbling his way towards the hill
through mud and wreckage strewn across his path,
to get fresh water from a little spring
which issued from the rocks and trickled down.
And there, beside the spring, to his surprise
stood Chanui's pail, not thrown nor tossed aside,
but upright, filled with water, clear and sweet.

29. DREAMING

I see in your developing smile,
exquisite beings must people your dreams.
You will never tell me,
only that you can force yourself to wake
from nightmares.
Make me metamorphose
into those moments
where you escape
and I cannot follow.
Sleep again
and take me with you.

30. THE DIAMOND MUSEUM, BRUGES

Industrial diamonds wink and gleam
like dewdrops shafted with sun.
If you could only sift them
like beach soft sand
to produce firework phosphorescence
again and again!

For lovers of geometry
there is spider-web fascination
in faceted patterns,
depths of cave mirrored pools,
captured rainbows.

31. THE BURNING EYE

Our elders do not know the reason why
we suffer problems from the burning eye.
It shrivels all our crops this time of year.
The lack of food is hard for us to bear.
Perhaps they'll save a little; even so
we're hungry till the Autumn berries show.

But then sometimes it goes away so long
in Winter, that the elders fear our song
is powerless to bring it back at need,
to ripen grain, once we have scattered seed.
They plan to build an altar from the stones,
empower it by using human bones.

I hate the rainstorms and the thunder's noise.
That's when they choose among the stronger boys
by making them draw lots. It's useless then
to hope for any mercy from the men.
I fear the chieftain with his blood-stained knife.
I fear he'll come among us for a life.

32. SUMMER SNAPSHOT

Circling yachts, burdened with bright sails,
catch the sun.
Children kneel in the sand.
Grandfather, in the only deckchair,
sits shaded by knotted handkerchief.
The ladies, tennis-racquets in hand
are poised to escape the camera,
while father, sporting binoculars,
gazes wistfully at the cliffs.
No one has noticed the Pekingese
cocking its leg against
the splintering chalet steps.

33. "ALL THAT GLISTERS"...

Light spreads across the surface of the lake.
It burnishes the ripples as they flow
to meet each margin with a soft caress.
A heron lurks, concealed within the reeds;
remorselessly, he stabs at passing fish.

Light jewels stones on the cathedral floor,
ignites a brass "In loving memory"
but cannot raise the occupant beneath.
A toddler swoops to wrest a coloured hoard
and fails to understand his empty hands.

Light filters through the forest canopy,
illuminates and flickers on the ferns.
Young horses heave and pant between the trees,
their breath suspended on the morning air.
The forest stirs and starts another day.
Light arcs the sky with promises of God.
There's legend of largesse at rainbow's end.
where treasure lies beneath the subtle hues.
Excitement fires a wish to hold and keep
this loveliness of transitory light.

34. DOWN THE YARD

My schoolfriend's gran was stout and old.
She sang quite loud, off-key.
But when I was a little girl
I often went to tea.

She had a cottage with a well.
We fetched the water in
and volunteered to feed the hens
with barley from the bin.

And in return she baked us buns
or gave us other treats
like special toffee-apples
or lovely home-made sweets.

The only thing that I disliked
was going down the yard
to a hut with dim, sepulchral light
whose wooden seat was hard.

It had three holes cut side by side,
One large one and two small
and, being quite petite, I felt
that I was sure to fall

down in the noxious mixture there
below us in the tank,
like my blue hair slide slipped and fell
and very slowly sank

right out of sight of all of us,
my friend, her brother, me.
You see there's strength in numbers
when you're going out to tea.

35. MARSH

Marsh seeps seawards,
oozes, squelches,
Oystercatcher prints
pattern the surface
like criss-crossed racquet strings.

Underneath,
it globs and gurgles,
leading the unwary
to the place
where water-channels
give way
to sucking, glutinous mud.

Stray wellington boots
tell their own tale.

36. THE FIRST CHRISTMAS

In the hay a baby sleeps.
By his side his mother weeps.
Though she has exceeding joy
from the arrival of this boy,
something makes her catch her breath,
gives premonition of his death.
But above the animal sounds
an angel choir sings all around
and shepherds kneel in awestruck gaze,
then stammer out their simple praise.
Above the byre, the star shines bright
dispensing its ethereal light.
It guides the splendid eastern kings,
with phials and tubs of precious things.
We see one doff his diadem
in the stable there at Bethlehem.

Each person brought whatever he could
to lay at the feet of the new, young Lord.
So give your gifts, both large and small
and think of that first Christmas of all.

37. VICTIM

Target rings around your eyes
mean unsettled sleep,
hair erect in hedgehog spines
that you cannot cope.
As fingers scrabble mouse-like,
trembling body shakes
with effort, in your struggle
to articulate
the sufferings which afflict
you. I make a guess,
fearing what you recollect.
Drop all squeamishness
and speak to me, **lest I miss
beyond the mind's wall**
your perceptible distress.

(excerpt in bold from *"On the Sea Wall"* by Ted Walker)

38. MEETING

No need to wait for Dear Mama
to furnish us a chaperone.
We now secrete ourselves away,
make trysts by e-mail or by phone.

39. ENDING

He writhes and scrabbles as he fights for life
while locked in pain. His body lingers on.
No further purpose in the surgeon's knife,
for just a husk remains. His mind has gone.
He strains and struggles to communicate.
We strive to understand, but cannot know
his tortured mind's processes. Human fate
is worse than dogs and cats must undergo.
Wild shouts and plaintive moans disturb his peace.
Then drugs enforce a silence no one can
achieve in other ways. But his decease
will, after all, reveal him as a man.
Maybe the Inuit had the right idea
to choose their moment to depart from here.

40. MIRACLE FLOWERS

The bloom on my fingers
carries the scent
of freesias.
I swallow,
gulp down their heady perfume,
like evening on the breeze.

Blue and white tablecloths
carry vases of yellow blooms.
Beside the three-tier cake,
my bride's bouquet,
maidenhair fern,
white and yellow freesias,
miracle flowers in December
throw Spring sunshine
into our lives,
promising fulfilment.

41. PERUVIAN SCISSOR DANCE

His giant scissors clash like castanets.
The halves, held separately, seem more like spears.
They stir the crowd, which moves to give him space.
Occasionally he holds a coloured scarf
and keeps his hands at all times off the floor.
The oval, patterned hat the dancer wears,
is like a shaman's mask, conceals his face.
It menaces, despite its rainbow hue
and ribbons floating freely from the side.
His shirt is white, with leg-of-mutton sleeves,
topped by embroidered waistcoat, while fur chaps
conceal his shorts, protect his legs and knees.
Both violin and harp attend this dance,
gymnastic movements done at lightning speed.
He somersaults, does head and shoulder stands,
in splits-position bounces cross the floor.
He's up on toe-point next, then on his back,
repeating movements, spinning round and round.

Tradition holds that these are ritual skills
compacted with the devil long ago.
He's menacing in ways one can't explain
and crowds retreat, scared by elusive threats.

42. DETECTIVE WORK

It's love some say,
interpreting
the twinkles in the eye.
But only he and she know
whether there'll be a blessing
or whether they'll keep us guessing.

43. SEASCAPE

Hot, wet sand crunches,
sticks beneath my tender feet,
lies in crevices.

Seaweed-smelling surf,
deliciously cooling foam,
reaches my bare knees.

Warily watchful
adults, sun-tanned, lethargic,
attempt to doze. Young

children tirelessly
excavating in rock pools
shriek exciting finds!

Donkeys, like ancient
Methuselah, plod, weary,
without complaining.

Seagulls call, strident,
disputing food and crying
loud imprecations.

Strange peace to my ears,
forever representing
a seaside morning.

44. CAPILLA REAL

What royalty could match for pomp
the statues' painted likenesses
revered before the altar-face?
Yet Ferdinand and Isabelle
lie calmly in simplicity
secreted in the crypt below
in coffins shorn of ornament.

45. MAKE-UP GIRL

She treats us to a side show on the train,
applying make-up, talking on the phone,
"I'm sorry, sorry, sorry. No it's me!"

She first applies a slash of vulval red,
meanwhile her flatvoiced murmur carries on
repeating "Sorry, sorry. No it's me!"

Eye shadow follows in coal-scuttle black,
Egyptian Kohl too heavily applied
reminding me of boxers in the ring.

She sprinkles sparkles onto half-closed lids
but just as fast obliterates them all,
which makes it clear to what extent she's cried.

She dabs some heavy blusher on her cheeks,
delineates each lip with pencil gloss,
then castigates herself with her refrain.

The train pulls in the station and she leaves
the guilt of "Sorry, sorry. No it's me!"
Behind her in the carriage there's a sigh.

We feel some empathy, a fleeting wish
that very soon indeed he'll understand.
Yet sadly the enigma still remains.

46. THE BEGINNINGS OF AN ADDICTION

Secreted in the lavatory,
blunt pencil in hand,
I'd draw for my small playmate
on toilet paper
the family referred to
as IZZAL GHIRMITHIDE
from my first lisping attempts.
Only a short while
before a voice would enquire,
"Just what are you doing in there?"

Progressing to Thankyous
in coloured crayons
on various offcuts.
Later, trying to control my words
over thick, black guidelines,
or sending for information
from magazines.

I felt important
with my present of Queen's Velvet
plus Dad's old fountain pen.
But sometimes the nib dug
like a spearpoint,
and the occasional spider
tiptoed over the paper
leaving his shadowed imprint.
I would tut and mutter,
tear the page and start again.

THE CLOSING OF THE ROSE

Dry, clean, like silk under the fingers,
pristine, enticing,
No sheet of paper remained
unblemished for long.
I was eager to send letters,
anticipating the delight of a return,
but wary lest the post-box mouth
bite my small fingers.

Today, in the drawer of my desk
I found your letter from years ago
stuck limpet-fashion
to the bottom of a box.
I have sought those loving words
in my frailer moments,
turned out bags and boxes,
raked through the loft,
scrabbled through ancient pockets.
How often I have needed your support,
a hand to steady me in my endeavour,
longing for your wrap-around words
to keep me safe.

Now you're here again,
my gladness flares
like glowing sparks
in the blackest of night skies.

47. REBIRTH

(after 'Metamorphosis of Narcissus', Salvador Dali)

Narcissus slumps,
by the pool, head on knee;
no longer self-admiring,
no longer even thinking,
drained of all emotion.

A sulphurous egg stench gathers,
takes on form.
Dead hand conjures
a gently balanced egg.

Lightning splits the clouds,
cracks the shell.
Like a damp butterfly
his petalled imago emerges.

The crowd spots nothing,
not even the Devil ready to spawn.
Indifferent to their chessboard fate
they gather gossiping.
Hell is not supposed to have miracles.

48. A MINUTE MYSTERY

He drops his toy to take a bite
and gets a fright
when doorbell rings.
Her toddler clings
as mother slaves to still his cries,
suppress her sighs.
She's almost sure
it's kids next door.
The door, when opened, then displays
to startled gaze
no more than air.
There's no one there!

49. ARIES, the Ram

I curl my lip and toss my head in scorn
at human beings, with their posturings,
I, Aries, brother to the dazzling gods
of Ancient Egypt, where on pyramid walls,
their legends lie encrypted. You will note
my stout, substantial, ridged and curling horns
bear witness to my fearsome ancestry;
Ra's cousin, he who wore the solar disc
and travelled nightly in his golden barque
through chasmic waters in the Underworld.
We met against the brutish ones below.
We stood by Hathor, Lady of the West,
and fought ferociously, successive nights,
so Ra could safely journey West to East
to bring the world the newness of the dawn.
I Aries, brother to the god Khnum
who was creator of your human race,
I influence them, more subtly than they know.

50. TAURUS – the bull

Down on the farm with the bullocks and cows in it,
there by the stream is a shed with a door
fastened by rope; and a window, no glass to it
where I would stand and I'd bellow so sore.

Mother was gentle and calm on the face of it.
Father was champion bull at the show.
Follow your father and fight where there's need of it.
This is the way for young bullocks to go.

I have a brother whose mind is made up to it –
All that he craves is just cutting a dash
inside a china shop, dreaming I'm sure of it,
ways of creating a glorious smash.

All that I want is some land with good grass on it,
not to be shut in a shed all the time,
clover and daisies and buttercups sweet in it
scattered in grass, in a field that is mine.

If a man climbs through a fence on the edge of it,
if he's not careful, he'll make me irate.
If he wears red and I don't like the hue of it,
I'll toss him suddenly over the gate.

I'm not so bad that I want him to hurt for it.
I just get cross when I'm here on my own,
hoping that things will get better. I'll see to it
when the cows come and I'm no more alone.

51. GEMINI – the twins

Source of love and jealousy,
my brother is another me,
born as twins, alike as can be.
People are unsure who they see.

They sometimes call me 'What's-your-name'
and for my brother it's much the same.
But as adults we'll grow our own fame.
At least that is our stated aim.

For now, it's as if we share one face.
We swop our selves, end in disgrace,
then hide and chuckle and embrace.
This game of ours is commonplace.

There's sometimes a bad atmosphere
when we compete. That's crystal-clear.
But I am mostly glad he's here
and all my life will hold him dear.

52. CANCER – the crab

Beady eyes glare at me
with unusual concentration,
mixed with malevolence
because I turn the stones,
exposing his hiding place.
Excelling at concealment,
he leaves his carapace behind,
pretends to be a whelk.

We would eagerly copy,
but fear exposure
of our soft inner core.
Deftly, we build yearly layers.

53. LEO – the lion

The kings of Egypt took my strength,
my bones insurance in their tombs,
while I as Sphinx, stood faithful guard
to point their starry path to heaven.
I faced the dragon in Hong Kong,
its claws like scythes and dripping blood,
while evil breath sought my demise.
Yet it survived to bear their shield.

And now, for generations here,
the English monarchs have me stand
together with the unicorn.
His horn is gold, his coat is white.
A coronet adorns his throat,
its price a chained captivity.
I'm royally crowned and standing free
to roar aloud in their defence.

I'm fiercely savage, regal, real
with thickened pelt and flowing mane.
I'll spring and launch a fierce attack.
Just fiction lets my rivals thrive.
So, if you gaze up to the heavens
one glowing, moonlit, cloudless night,
you'll see I've earned my due reward
and set my pathway to the stars.

54. VIRGO – the virgin

You see, Mary, he's good at using tools
to smooth the wood and making joints to fit
and gauging sizes using wooden rules.
He'll follow me and make a job of it.

But, Joseph, have you asked him what he feels?
    He's thinking for himself now he has grown,
    not simply stating what he has been taught.
    I cannot see him making wooden wheels!
    Somehow his longings are a bit high-flown
    and he's expressing complicated thoughts.

I've told your mother you should have this trade.
We've customers galore who need things done.
Look Jesus, take a pride in what you've made
and learn the way my business here is run.

But I have God the Father's work to do.
    I must dispute the doctrines of the Law
    and teach his way of love to those I meet.
    He wants us to consider things anew,
    to love and help the suffering and the poor
    and give our thanks in reverence at his feet.

You've heard the lad. I think I understand.
He won't be bound in simple lives like ours.
I've felt God's minion take me by the hand
and known the consummation of his powers.

Yet I still fear for Jesus, for all men
    have jealousy and evil in their hearts.
    He should not pit himself against their might.
    But who am I to argue with him when
    he's sure the messages that he imparts
    will turn the world away from dark, to light?

55. LIBRA – the scales

Imagination's child lies bawling in the scales.
He sails, pro tem, above the knowledge
that his father weaves an unsteady path,
his mother is a lady of the streets.
He will start with a level balance however.
For only his deeds will be recorded
in the Book of Life
and his heart weighed against the Feather of Truth.

56. SCORPIO – the scorpion

You can creep like a thief
but beware should your footfall
disturb his sleep in the sand.
His hard segmented body springs up,
tail aloft like a proud puppy.
If you avoid his pincers
the poisoned thorn in his tail
will give you repeated torments.
How was this image
burned in Ezekiel's brain?
Had he seen someone thrown
in a pit of scorpions
for punishment or revenge?

Soft as jelly, we can only suffer,
But the brave mongoose
crunches him up,
sting and all.

57. SAGITTARIUS – the archer

A ccuse me of mere boasting if you will.
R ough boys don't just develop such a skill
C ommanding movements of the hand and eye.
H is lordship wants to know the reason why
E vading practice seems to be so smart.
R eal archery's a clever, dextrous art.

58. CAPRICORN – The goat

Agile as dancers
ibex leap from rock to rock
high in Tibet.
With horns like locked swords,
they wrestle for higher ground
to dominate the scene.
For us, gulping the thin air
is seizing the nothingness of candyfloss,
but even sparse vegetation
sustains their verve and virility.

Prayer flags crack in the breeze.
The goatherd has a new son.
Give thanks to Buddha, the monks say.
His neighbours mix flour and butter,
make flour-ibex which they bring
the family to celebrate the child.
Centuries old, this tradition
conveys to the baby
the animals' fleet footedness
in hard terrain,
its stamina and strength.

59. AQUARIUS – the water carrier

Not the male of legend
but figure of fact,
tasting dust which turns
her yellow-patterned clothing grey,
An African mother sways home
bringing water from the lake.
In her headgear, folded to a neat nest,
sits a large plastic petrol can.
She's footsore, trudging half the day
under concrete weight,
skin dry as cracked parchment,
from blazing sun.
One hand carries a bowl
to catch escaping drips.
Even these are precious,
for this chore needs repeating
like a penance, each foreseeable tomorrow,
if they are to drink.
Yet this water of life
has life-forms
which may themselves bring death.

60. PISCES – the fish

Anchovy, haddock, cod, plaice or jack,
catch them and measure them. Throw a few back.

Lemon sole, velvetfish, yellowtail, tench,
the largest will give your line a good wrench.

Quillfish and parrotfish, mackerel and ide
are all borne along by fresh current, or tide.

Sturgeon and flounder, wrasse dab and eel,
what can beat fish for an excellent meal!

61. PORTRAIT OF EDITH SITWELL

Head inclined,
she struts forward,
each arrow glance
questioning one's presence.

Long thin fingers
twitter at her sides,
unease persisting
since clumsy childhood days.

A toque conceals
greying hair,
once spun green-gold thread
matching her green-eyed piercing stare.

She stands central,
apart,
her poetry a bulwark
against vulnerability
or further hurt.

62. NO ANSWER

Grief's cauldron
simmers,
never boils dry.
Memory forces seethe and overflow.
That day
scalds my mind
a quarter-century gone.

Small, helpless babe,
declining to breathe,
whose life might have been anguished,
Why am I surprised
you still lie
under my heart,
my love untarnished?

63. LIGHTHOUSE KEEPER

Even blanket thickness is not enough
to deter the wind.
He takes his lamp
beyond shelter
of the lighthouse,
while wind gnaws his ankles,
tugs at duffel-fastenings,
sneaks through fibres
to chill his chest.

It brings smells
of seaweed and fish
to assail his nostrils,
overlaying everything,
before and after shave the same.

On wild days,
stepping out for a box of stores
means assault
by the wind's force,
feeling his ears buffeted,
as formerly
by his mother's avenging hand.

Gnarled features
top a thick-knit sweater.
His hands look grimy
with ingrained cracks;
sandpaper rope-handles
abrade his fingers
that relish the smoothness
of polished lamp-glass.

THE CLOSING OF THE ROSE

He tastes
salt on his tongue,
sand and grit
in the relentless wailing wind
which whirls waves,
dumping tons of water
a few feet from the door.

He envies
gulls
soaring above
mountainous seas
and awaits calmer times
to spy inquisitive seals.

Within the lighthouse
is a certain cosiness.
Cramped confinement
brews storms
between the best of friends,
irritated beyond endurance
by something simple
as a cough.

In spare minutes,
he carves and paints,
a red and white replica lighthouse,
home for his heart
and his life's work.

64. ARCTIC EXPLORER

Fingers like brass stair-rods, now unbending,
glazed eyes fixed by the relentless glare,
urine frozen as it splashes earthward;
he joined the survey largely for a dare.

Macho image thrust on adolescence,
soon he dodged his mother's fond embrace.
Fame was dangled as the bait before him.
Now he knows he'll reach no other place.

Trudging knee-deep in the fallen snowdrifts,
strength will fade before he reaches base,
stumbling wildly as a jerking puppet.
Ice is setting, smothering his face.

Now his elegant, ambitious girlfriend,
eager for her moment of shared fame,
will not see beyond the awful headlines,
know he died while whispering her name.

65. JUNKIE

Eyes clouded with drugs,
he sits and whines for change,
like Rover for his bone.
Who sees the humanity beneath his blanket,
or the devastated lives in his wake?

66. AFTERMATH

Emotions chase over your face
like the wind on a lawn.
You smile to yourself, then frown
and what was pleasure
turns and is gone.

Beyond that, as I watch, unseen
I see you journey through your brain
to the old affair.
Only time can refine
the lines of the grief we've borne.

Yet I thank God I'm here.
You're not alone.

67. ELEMENTAL PRAYER

EARTH   Cherish the footprints
of the mud-pie makers.
Their stay will not be long.

AIR   Cradle the thistledown
gently above the sails.
For storms are too strong.

FIRE   Tame your burning core
to comfort frost-dwellers.
Keep them safe nightlong.

WATER   Sustain our lives.
Let your waterfalls
gladden us with their song.

68. LANGUOR

blazing glints of golden sunlight
breaking beams on wavelets
clouds look fringed in fuzzy outlines
trees tinged as if fire lit

watch the locals silent sailing
languid lengthened shadows
we make note from marine escarpments
ranged remote in meadows

69. CALLING ARTHUR

"Come, take me up. My blade is whetted keen
to serve the rightful king; and how the sheen
attracts usurpers! My encrusted jewels
will serve you, Arthur, not that host of fools.
Trapped in this stone, I hide my wondrous length
and only magic will give you the strength
to draw me out. I languish here unused.
My powers and your goodness shall be fused.
Come, Arthur, take me up. My blade is keen
to serve the rightful king. Change what has been.

Hold high my hilt before the godless horde.
They shall, through your example, love the Lord.
Childric's defeat will bring you lands once lost
to strife and chaos. It shall be your boast
that love and order follow in your wake.
Your knights shall strive and battle for your sake.
Hold high my hilt. The diamonds' flashing glance
will pain your foes as sorely as a lance.

Shout out the bold inscription on my blade.
Antagonists will fight, but be afraid.
From Caerleon-on-Usk we'll go to Rome
to keep the foreign armies from our home.
And, as we pass, take me to Michael's Mount
to slay the giant there. He cannot daunt
your fervour. My sharp blade will run him through
and end his loathsome reputation too.
Shout out the bold inscription on my blade.
They'll recognise the magic Merlin made.

THE CLOSING OF THE ROSE

And when, through Mordred's treachery, you're slain
and cannot set me in the stone again,
then take me to the mere and throw me in.
There will be other fights for me to win.
The lady's hand will catch and draw me down.
Through centuries they'll hear of our renown.
But, rest assured, some future king will heed
and draw Excalibur in England's need."

70. AUERSPERG CONCERT

Pink and green marble,
soft ballet-slipper footfalls,
diamond-patterned floor.
I expect the Rosenkavalier
to spring in,
silver-rose between his teeth;
in powdered wig and frock-coat
to whirl me round the floor.
The orchestra's verve
will tempt figures from the frieze
to waltz in their turn.
Crystal chandeliers ring
with the mezzo-soprano's voice
and her emotion.

Melodies sing in my head
long after the music has died.
The mind revolves
and my eyes dazzle
after the last beat's fading.

71. DAYBREAK

The soft-shoed sun creeps through a curtain-crack
with morning admonitions to forewarn
of likely vengeance still to come. It's not
the reason I am loath to see this dawn.

Last night we scattered clothing round the room.
Bright daylight shows its furnishings are worn,
not noticed in our haste, but not the cause
of my unwillingness to view the dawn.

Her raven hair lies draped along my arm.
Her honeyed skin has beauty some would scorn.
I foresee problems here, but nothing which
would make me dread to see the breaking dawn.

Her safety from pursuit falls to my charge.
I love her with my life. That's what I've sworn
and now I need my plan to work. Of course
I'm much unsettled by this coming dawn.

72. SEA-SENSE

Birds dart and swoop the waves
capturing attention.
Netted fish and seaweed
invade my nostrils.
Lines tinkle and slap the masts
while the sea
pounds the pebbles
forever.
Warm sand buries my toes.
Salt tangs my tongue
savouring the sandwiches.
I feel more alive by the sea.

73. WAIL

Rail-safety is of paramount concern.
It grieves us that they're always much too late
repairing defects, so we can't discern
Rail safety is of paramount concern.
The relatives of those who won't return
wished firms would act, not just reiterate
"Rail safety is of paramount concern."
It grieves us that they're always much too late.

74. IMPRINT

She has the wide smile of Eve's daughter
and eyes that are springing with laughter;
no feminine attribute missing,
created for hugging and kissing.
Who is this redoubtable lady?
Why, woman of course, stupid, said he.

75. BLUE HILLS REMEMBERED

Based on a true occurrence

Shep, off his lead, was frightened by the cars.
He hated all the noise, the steaming fumes
that overlay his dainty sense of smell.
He knew that he belonged below the hills
where space was plentiful with many fields.
The sheep on Clapham Common did not stir
from steady munching. They were left to graze
for hours upon this public plot of land
and juicy grass filled all their vacant thoughts.
But Shep, a collie visiting the town
could see they were neglected, straying loose.
Since puppyhood in Wales he surely knew
that sheep could not be left to go their way,
to straggle, panic, lose themselves at will.
They needed to be kept within the flock
and driven where the shepherd wanted them.
Remembering he'd helped his mother chase
at bullet speed across the grassy slopes
of high blue hills, which disappeared again
into the mist with dusk, or dawn's light haze,
to gather all the sheep within her range,
he knew his task. Before he was recalled,
or given any signal of command
he'd herded them into a single group
and, crouching, kept them bunched beneath a tree.

76. IN THE TEAHOUSE

Red fish circle
in blood-red hollyhock shadow.
Waterlily pad shudders
to frog leap.
In the teahouse
the garden's designer watches
leaf-plopping rain.
Only the bullfrogs
mar his peace.

77. DENIAL

She hears him pace the floor. He cannot sleep.
His footsteps seem to move about all night.
Were he a woman, she is sure he'd weep

upon her shoulder, tell her of his plight.
But nothing seems to help his sorry state.
She knows that what is happening will blight

his life; and possibly they'd deprecate
it, if they knew the truth. Therefore he frowns
and mutters to himself, descries his fate.

He has already moved through several towns.
The neighbours do not want him anywhere.
He hides behind the curtains and he downs

far too much whisky. But they do not care
that this will make him ill; they daily hope
that he will move, so they no longer bear

his night-time noises. For they cannot cope
with what he might suggest, by crying "Why?...
That girl! It wasn't me." They fix a rope
outside. It's certain he won't mollify
their wrath. Unless he goes, they'll hang him high.

78. GRANDAD'S WORKSHOP

Remember pushing through the door,
ankle deep in shavings,
paper-thin spirals of wood
like Goldilock's curls?
One corner is mysterious;
windows blanked out by whitewash
to defend the stored wood
from thieves.
I scratch peepholes
and infant pictures anyway.

But what hits you is the smell,
new timber and fishy glue;
perspiring men,
sweat running in lines
to splash in the sawdust underfoot.

Escaping into the yard,
I echo the hammer's rhythm
as I pat the sand
to shape castles and caves;
I revel in the noises
the adults hate.
The saw teeth seem to be singing.

79. HASTINGS

Pebbles crunch
below East Hill.
Two white-haired fishermen
perch on rickety chairs
beside a shed door. Shifting weight,
gazing to the far horizon's cloud-blurred,
gull-mobbed boats,
they pause,
smile and reminisce.
Draped from climbing wall height
on the boarded door
is a rust coloured net
they are mending.
Their sons' livelihoods are woven
in their expertise,
as they thread and tug knots in line
like the knit one, purl one of their guernseys.
Fifteen years back
they, too, fought the sea each day
taking its treasures.
Now, pickings are slimmer,
danger the same. They worry
whether their grandsons will be inveigled
by the tug of the wind.

80. ARTFUL DODGER

Red Admiral
swoops, darts, banks, turns
crazily on thin air
frantic to arrive
but just exactly where?
He angles aimlessly,
unsighting pursuing swallow
in the sun's glare.

81. EVENING MIST, HEIAN

Paper lanterns in subtle hues,
gardens shadowed in misty blues,
as Heian is lost in the mist.
Who will appear from the darkness there,
caught by a lantern's sudden flare,
a lady illicitly kissed?
Then the lovers vanish again
as we peer through the murk in vain
for a glimpse of Heian through the mist.

82. COMING OUT

Maturing new ideas like brewing wine,
Imagining a body in the blocked
Carrara marble, prisoned from our sight;
He hews and pecks and grinds the stubborn stone,
Excises stone-chips, coaxes out the form,
Lets loose great David's beauty on the world.
Among the crowd, stone-throwers who respond,
Not with his pleasure in the nubile curves
Gracing the silk-smooth buttocks. He admires
Each facet of the figure; gazes up,
Laments that his creation cannot love,
Outclassing all the world's apprentice boys.

83. GREAT GRANDMA, LOUISA

Never out of her chair
she hunched in the corner, to glare,
subjecting all to scrutiny,
failing to spot undercurrents of mutiny.

Filled with frissons of fear,
her grandchildren felt, every year,
that visiting was no pleasure.
They had other ideas of spending their leisure.

But, dressed in Sunday best,
we were somehow put to the test
and all of us taken to tea
ignoring the prospect of childhood misery.

In Victorian black,
forbidding, with her ramrod back
and full of don'ts, she would command
obedience and issue forth demands.

Don't scratch the furniture.
You will soon feel my displeasure
and mind your head against the wall
or you will not be welcome here at all.

It cannot be denied,
she may have had a pleasant side,
but she kept us children at bay
and we very quickly wanted to get away.

84. NARRATIVE

Little lambs are brought bleating from the hills.
Child cries, curled in the manger.
Shepherds struggle the dire distance,
a weary walk to wintry Bethlehem
>   but yet
>   We hear their tale again –
>   In blaze of evening sunset,
>   snow, hail or blinding rain
>   and never ever forget.

Kings with crowns, robes of royal red
bring boxes, gaily glittering gold.
Camels carry them, mincing many miles.
Awkward animals stumble and spit
>   but yet
>   We hear the tale again –
>   In blaze of evening sunset,
>   snow, hail or blinding rain
>   and never ever forget.

Awe-inspiring angels lull barefoot baby.
Soaring songs still watchers to silence.
Everyone kneels, knowing nothing
of what they should beware,
>   but yet
>   We hear their tale again –
>   In blaze of evening sunset,
>   Snow, hail or blinding rain.
>   We wish you peace again
>   so never ever forget.

THE CLOSING OF THE ROSE

85. WILDE GENIUS

Late nineteenth century
poet, playwright and aesthete,
Oscar's intellectual plane
surpassed every scholar he was likely to meet.

Despite his biting wit
he was a sensitive soul,
yet carrying a lily
through a London street, regarded as rather droll.

Throughout his life he mourned
his young sister's childhood death.
He carried her lock of hair
and extolled pursuit of beauty, with every breath.

At Oxford and beyond
he earned a reputation
for eccentric brilliance
in his decorative tastes and conversation.

First he published poems,
then children's stories and plays,
but courted controversy
with his novel "The Picture of Dorian Gray."

Considered immoral,
it caused a deal of protest,
its homoerotic tone
allied to the reasons for his later arrest.

THE CLOSING OF THE ROSE

His wife disowned his name
and took their children abroad
while he spent time in prison,
no chance of his reputation being restored.

He died, aged forty-six
in Paris, a destitute,
still knowing that here at home
he would be regarded as being dissolute.

Today, his plays live on.
We like the social satire
and his literary skills
expressed in many ways, are something we desire.

"Drift with every passion"
was his credo, come what may.
He suffered for his choices
but would be viewed with greater tolerance today.

86. NUDE BATHING

Multiple loops of river,
patterned like a wrought-iron balustrade,
cut through rainforest.
Mighty Congo Basin diminishes
to a Thames girdle,
shallows to waist-deep tributaries.
In larger, calmer stretches
a barge tows the river market,
screened stalls bearing wooden basins,
and colourful cloths.
Propelled by a single oar,
long, narrow canoes glide
under forest canopy.
Away from disturbance, a man stands
knee-deep, throwing a hand-net.
Small, nude boys,
hurl themselves in,
to dive for tourist coins,
or just from mere exhuberance.

87. THE BIRTH OF VENUS

(Botticelli)

The peach-skin caressing
scallop-bearing sea
longs for Venus to step in.
It floats her ashore,
not cradled in foetal curl
but adult,
upright as a poplar.
Zephyrs blow her gently to land
in a flurry of pink succulents.
Her skin is alabaster,
baby perfect
yet her eyes hold Eve's knowledge.
So, Venus too, covers her womanhood,
but with a cascade of golden hair.
Offered a cloak
for her nakedness,
she remains impassive,
unhurried, self-possessed;
Adonis must wait.
His time will come.

THE CLOSING OF THE ROSE

88. RECIDIVIST

For three months now, he'd stood this freezing hell,
no bed to cradle weary bones at night;
not even four walls of a prison cell
secured him from the pavement's vicious bite.
His bedroll grew much heavier each day.
He trudged from door to doorway through the streets
to hear repeatedly "Just go away!
Our neighbourhood can do without dead-beats!"
A woman passed by, looking rather frail.
He grabbed her bag, just as she saw the knife.
This time they wouldn't let him out on bail.
This time the judge would sentence him to 'life'.
He told a mate, "I'm sorry that she died,"
but still he thought 'At least it's warm inside.'

89. STAR CREDENTIALS

In infancy, we float the starstream,
glow from Ara to Orion,
hide night's secrets in stardust.

Juniors slide the sky's chenille,
spin and scintillate like ice-dancers,
cartwheel on five points.

Catapulting teenagers shoot
at bullet-speed
flaring the heavens.
Harder still, we learn
a ballet-dancer's absolute stillness,
allowing humans to navigate.

Trained adults
sparkle the Earth,
jewel sapphires
and return to rest,
off-shift, on the clouds.

The glitterati
become lodestars,
or even supergiants.
I'm destined to fill a vacancy
this December, over Bethlehem.

90. PEOPLE

Tony Blair
took the Chair
of the meeting
with only the elite in.

Sir Alec Rose
chose
to circumnavigate the world
with his sails unfurled.

Peter Abelard
found life very hard.
But Heloise, denied him,
was buried beside him.

Alfred, the Great,
in 878
forced the Danes to retreat
and caused their defeat.

Fred Astaire
seemed lighter than air
as he danced.
We were entranced.

THE CLOSING OF THE ROSE

James Clerk Maxwell
wandering the Cambridge Backs, fell
in discussion with Faraday one night,
said, "Let's develop electric light."

Edmund Clerihew Bentley
pleaded, "Please treat me gently!
I did not invent the form
to kick up a storm."